Marriage

✦

A Celebration

Marriage

A Celebration

LORENZ BOOKS

NEW YORK • LONDON • SYDNEY • BATH

✢

This edition published in 1997 by Lorenz Books
27 West 20th Street, New York NY 10011

LORENZ BOOKS are available for bulk purchase, for sales promotion and for
premium use. For details write or call the manager of special sales:
Lorenz Books, 27 West 20th Street, New York NY 10011; (800) 354-9657.

© 1997 Anness Publishing Limited

Lorenz Books is an imprint of Anness Publishing Limited

ISBN 1 85967 398 8

Publisher: Joanna Lorenz
Project Editor: Joanne Rippin
Text researched by: Steve Dobell
Illustrations by: Lucy Pettifer
Designer: Andrew Heath

Printed and bound in China

1 3 5 7 9 10 8 6 4 2

Contents

❧

CHAPTER ONE

The Greatest of These is Love

*I*t is a truth universally acknowledged, that a single man in possession of a good fortune must be in want of a wife. However little known the feelings or views of such a man may be on his first entering a neighbourhood, this truth is so well fixed in the minds of the surrounding families, that he is considered as the rightful property of some one or other of their daughters.

"My dear Mr Bennet," said his lady to him one day, "have you heard that Netherfield Park is let at last?" Mr Bennet replied that he had not. "But it is," returned she; "for Mrs Long has just been here, and she told me all about it." Mr Bennet made no answer. "Do not you want to know who has taken it?" cried his wife impatiently. "You want to tell me, and I have no objection to hearing it." This was invitation enough. "Why, my dear, you must know, Mrs Long says that Netherfield is taken by a young man of large fortune from the north of England; that he came down on Monday in a chaise and four to see the place, and was so much delighted with it that he agreed with Mr Morris immediately; that he is to take possession before Michaelmas, and some of his servants are to be in the house by the end of next week."

"What is his name?"

"Bingley."

"Is he married or single?"

"Oh! single, my dear, to be sure! A single man of large fortune; four or five thousand a year. What a fine thing for our girls!"

"How so? How can it affect them?"

"My dear Mr Bennet..."

JANE AUSTEN
Pride and Prejudice

A-courting then Petruchio went to Katharine the Shrew, and first of all he applied to Baptista, her father, for leave to woo his gentle daughter Katharine, as Petruchio called her, saying archly, that having heard of her bashful modesty and mild behaviour, he had come from Verona to solicit her love. Her father, though he wished her married, was forced to confess Katharine would ill answer this character, it being soon apparent of what manner of gentleness she was composed, for her music-master rushed into the room to complain that the gentle Katharine, his pupil, had broken his head with her lute for presuming to find fault with her performance; which, when Petruchio heard, he said, "It is a brave wench; I love her more than ever, and long to have some chat with her;" and hurrying the

old gentleman for a positive answer, he said, "My business is in haste, Signior Baptista, I cannot come every day to woo. You knew my father. He is dead, and has left me heir to all his lands, and goods. Then tell me, if I get your daughter's love, what dowry you will give with her."

CHARLES AND MARY LAMB
Tales from Shakespeare

"Is it possible that this stranger has now become everything to me," she asked herself, and immediately answered, "Yes, everything! He alone is now dearer to me than everything in the world." Prince Andrei came up to her with downcast eyes. "I have loved you from the very first moment I saw you. May I hope?" He looked at her and was struck by the serious impassioned expression of her face. Her face said: "Why ask? Why doubt what you cannot but know? Why speak, when words cannot express what one feels?" She drew near to him and stopped. He took her hand and kissed it. "Do you love me?"

"Yes, yes!" Natasha murmured as if in vexation. Then she sighed loudly and, catching her breath more and more quickly, began to sob. "What is it? What's the matter?"

"Oh, I am so happy!" she replied, smiled through her tears, bent over closer to him, paused for an instant as if asking herself whether she might, and then kissed him.

LEO TOLSTOY
War and Peace

Soon words enough had passed between them to decide their direction towards the comparatively quiet and retired gravel walk, where the power of conversation would make the present hour a blessing indeed, and prepare it for all the immortality which the happiest recollections of their own future lives could bestow. There they exchanged again those feelings and those promises which had once before seemed to secure everything, but which had been followed by so many, many years of division and estrangement. There they returned again into the past, more exquisitely happy, perhaps in their re-union, than when it had been first projected; more tender, more tried, more fixed in a knowledge of each other's character, truth, and attachment; more equal to act, more justified in acting.

JANE AUSTEN

Persuasion

At this point Kate ceased to attend. He saw after a little that she had been following some thought of her own, and he had been feeling the growth of something determinant even through the extravagance of much of the pleasantry, the warm transparent irony, into which their livelier intimacy kept plunging like a confident swimmer. Suddenly she said to him with extraordinary beauty: "I engage myself to you for ever."

The beauty was in everything, and he could have separated nothing – couldn't have thought of her face as distinct from the whole joy. Yet her face had a new light. "And I pledge you – I call God to witness! – every spark of my faith; I give you every drop of my life." That was all, for the moment, but it was enough, and it was almost as quiet as if it were nothing. They were in the open air, in an alley of the Gardens; the great space, which seemed to arch just then higher and spread wider for them, threw them back into deep concentration. They moved by common instinct to a spot, within sight, that struck them as fairly sequestered, and there, before their time together was spent, they had extorted from concentration every advance it could make them. They had exchanged vows and tokens, sealed their rich compact, solemnized, so far as breathed words and murmured sounds and lighted eyes and clasped hands could do it, their agreement to belong only, and to belong tremendously, to each other.

HENRY JAMES

The Wings of the Dove

feel sad when I don't see you. Be married, why won't you? And come to live with me. I will make you as happy as I can. You shall not be obliged to work hard; and when you are tired, you may lie in my lap and I will sing you to rest. I will play you a tune upon the violin as often as you ask and as well as I can; and leave off smoking, if you say so . . . I would always be very kind to you, I think, because I love you so well. I will not make you bring in wood and water, or feed the pig, or milk the cow, or go to the neighbours to borrow milk. Will you be married?

LETTER FROM A SUITOR
19th century America

CHAPTER TWO

With this Ring I Thee Wed

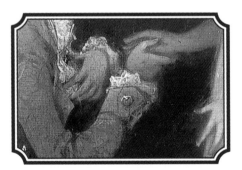

MARRIAGE

The joys of marriage are the heaven on earth,
Life's paradise, great princess, the soul's quiet,
Sinews of concord, earthly immortality,
Eternity of pleasures; no restoratives
Like to a constant woman.

JOHN FORD
The Broken Heart

23

*B*ehold while she before the altar stands,
  Hearing the holy priest that to her speaks,
And blesseth her with his two happy hands,
  How the red roses flush up in her cheeks,
And the pure snow, with goodly vermeil stain,
    Like crimson dyed in grain;
That even the Angels, which continually
  About the sacred altar do remain,
  Forget their service and about her fly,
Oft peeping in her face, that seems more fair
    The more they on it stare.

EDMUND SPENSER

"Epithalamion"

Theseus Now, fair Hippolyta, our nuptial hour
Draws on apace: four happy days bring in
Another moon; but O! methinks how slow
This old moon wanes; she lingers my desires,
Like to a step-dame, or a dowager
Long withering out a young man's revenue.

Hippolyta Four days will quickly steep themselves in night;
Four nights will quickly dream away the time;
And then the moon, like to a silver bow
New bent in heaven, shall behold the night
Of our solemnities.

Theseus Go, Philostrate,
Stir up the Athenian youth to merriments;
Awake the pert and nimble spirit of mirth;
Turn melancholy forth to funerals;
The pale companion is not for our pomp.
Hippolyta, I wooed thee with my sword,
And won thy love doing thee injuries;
But I will wed thee in another key,
With pomp, with triumph, and with revelling.

WILLIAM SHAKESPEARE
A Midsummer Night's Dream

The June roses over the porch were awake bright and early on that morning, rejoicing with all their hearts in the cloudless sunshine, like friendly little neighbours, as they were. Quite flushed with excitement were their ruddy faces, as they swung in the wind, whispering to one another what they had seen; for some peeped in at the dining-room windows, where the feast was spread, some climbed up to nod and smile at the sisters as they dressed the bride, others waved a welcome to those who came and went on various errands in garden, porch and hall, and all, from the rosiest full-blown flower to the palest baby-bud, offered their tribute of beauty and fragrance to the gentle mistress who had loved and tended them so long.

Meg looked very like a rose herself; for all that was best and sweetest in heart and soul seemed to bloom into her face that day, making it fair and tender, with a charm more beautiful than beauty. Neither silk, lace, nor orange-flowers would she have. "I don't want to look strange or fixed up today," she said. "I don't want a fashionable wedding, but only those about me whom I love, and to them I wish to look and be my familiar self."

So she made her wedding gown herself, sewing into it the tender hopes and innocent romances of a girlish heart. Her sisters braided up her pretty hair, and the only ornaments she wore were lilies-of-the-valley, which "her John" liked best of all the flowers that grew.

"You do look just like our own dear Meg, only so very sweet and lovely that I should hug you if it wouldn't crumple your dress," cried Amy, surveying her with delight, when all was done.

"Then I am satisfied. But please hug and kiss me, every one, and don't mind my dress; I want a great many crumples of this sort put into it today"; and Meg opened her arms to her sisters, who clung about her with April faces for a minute, feeling that the new love had not changed the old.

LOUISA M. ALCOTT

Good Wives

Then to the maiden's chamber maidens came,
And woke her up to love and joyous shame,
And as the merry sun streamed through the room
Spread out unequalled marvels of the loom,
Stored up for such an end in days long done,
Ere yet her grey eyes looked upon the sun;
Fine webs like woven mist, wrought in the dawn,
Long ere the dew had left the sunniest lawn,
Gold cloth so wrought that nought of gold seemed there,
But rather sunlight over blossoms fair;
You would have said that gods had made them, bright,
To hide her body from the common light
Lest men should die from unfulfilled desire.
Gems too they showed, wrought by the hidden fire
That eats the world, and from the unquiet sea
Pearls worth the ransom of an argosy.
Yet all too little all these riches seemed
In worship of her, who as one who dreamed,
By her fair maidens' hands was there arrayed,
Then, with loose hair, ungirded as a maid
Unto the threshold of the house was brought,
But when her hand familiar fingers caught
And when that voice, that erst amidst her fear
She deemed a god's, now smote upon her ear
Like one new-born to heaven she seemed to be.

WILLIAM MORRIS
The Earthly Paradise

*O*come, soft rest of cares! come, Night!
Come, naked Virtue's only tire,
The reaped harvest of the light
Bound up in sheaves of sacred fire.
Love calls to war:
Sighs his alarms,
Lips his swords are,
The field his arms.

Come, Night, and lay thy velvet hand
On glorious Day's outfacing face;
And all thy crowned flames command
For torches to our nuptial grace.
Love calls to war:
Sighs his alarms,
Lips his swords are,
The field his arms.

GEORGE CHAPMAN
"Bridal Song"

At length the happy day arrived, which was to put Joseph in the possession of all his wishes. He arose and dressed himself in a neat, but plain suit of Mr Booby's, which exactly fitted him; for he refused all finery; as did Fanny likewise, who could be prevailed on by Pamela to attire herself in nothing richer than a white dimity night-gown. Her shift indeed, which Pamela presented her, was of the finest kind, and had an edging of lace round the bosom; she likewise equipped her with a pair of fine white thread stockings, which were all she would accept; for she wore one of her own short round-eared caps, and over it a little straw hat, lined with cherry-coloured silk, and tied with a cherry-coloured ribbon. In this dress she came forth from her chamber, blushing and breathing sweets; and was by Joseph, whose eyes sparkled fire, led to church, the whole family attending, where Mr Adams performed the ceremony; (at which nothing was so remarkable, as the extraordinary and unaffected modesty of Fanny, unless the true Christian piety of Adams, who publicly rebuked Mr Booby and Pamela for laughing in so sacred a place, and so solemn an occasion).

HENRY FIELDING
The Adventures of Joseph Andrews

*H*ymen Then is there mirth in heaven,
When earthly things made even
     Atone together.
Good duke, receive thy daughter;
Hymen from heaven brought her;
     Yea, brought her hither,
That thou might'st join her hand with his,
     Whose heart within her bosom is.

*S*ong Wedding is great Juno's crown:
     O blessed bond of board and bed!
'Tis Hymen peoples every town;
     High wedlock then be honoured.
Honour, high honour, and renown,
To Hymen, god of every town!

WILLIAM SHAKESPEARE
As You Like It

Happily the sunshine fell more warmly than usual on the lilac tufts the morning that Eppie was married, for her dress was a very light one. She had often thought, though with a feeling of renunciation, that the perfection of a wedding dress would be a white cotton, with the tiniest pink sprig at wide intervals; so that when Mrs. Godfrey Cass begged to provide one, and asked Eppie to choose what it should be, previous meditation had enabled her to give a decided answer at once.

Seen at a little distance as she walked across the churchyard and down the village, she seemed to be attired in pure white, and her hair looked like the dash of gold on a lily. One hand was on her husband's arm, and with the other she clasped the hand of her father Silas.

"You won't be giving me away, father," she had said to him before they went to church; "you'll only be taking Aaron to be a son to you."

GEORGE ELIOT

Silas Marner

An almost universal feature of weddings is the wedding feast. It is one of the earliest ceremonies of marriage. In the Cyclades the feast lasted fifteen days, and the expenses were sometimes defrayed by the father of the bride, and sometimes by the bridegroom. Among the Navajos and the Burmese, eating together is the only ceremony; and it is the principal one among the Santals in Malay, and among the Hovas, Hindus, and Esthonians, as well as in Ermland, in Prussia, and in Sardinia. In Japan the drinking of cups of saki together is the most important part of the rite, and in Brazil brandy is the wedding drink. In Scandinavia the couple must drink from the same beaker.

This custom also survives in Christianity. It develops not merely into the wedding feast once universally shared by all the guests, but where the marriage service prescribes that the wedded couple should partake of the Sacrament together, the symbol of the "marriage supper of the Lamb", and this, strictly speaking, should not be omitted from any Christian wedding ceremony.

ETHEL L. URLIN
A Short History of Marriage

※

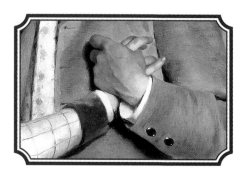

CHAPTER THREE

To Have and to Hold From this Day Forth

I consider a country dance as an emblem of marriage. Fidelity and complaisance are the principal duties of both; and those men who do not choose to dance or marry themselves have no business with the partners or wives of their neighbours. You will allow that in both man has the advantage of choice, woman only the power of refusal; that in both it is an engagement between man and woman, formed for the advantage of each; and that when once entered into, they belong exclusively to each other till the moment of its dissolution; that it is their duty each to endeavour to give the other no cause for wishing that he or she had bestowed themselves elsewhere, and their best interest to keep their own imaginations from wandering towards the perfections of their neighbours, or fancying that they should have been better off with any one else. . . . In one respect, there certainly is a difference. In marriage, the man is supposed to provide for the support of the woman; the woman to make the home agreeable to the man; he is to purvey and she is to smile. But in dancing, their duties are exactly changed: the agreeableness, the compliance, are expected from him, while she furnishes the fan and the lavender water.

JANE AUSTEN
Northanger Abbey

felt my life come back, and glow; I felt my trust in God revive; I felt the joy of living and of loving dearer things than life. It is not a moment to describe; who feels can never tell of it. But the compassion of my sweetheart's tears, and the caressing of my bride's lips, and the throbbing of my wife's heart *(now at last at home on mine)* made me feel that the world was good, and not a thing to be weary of.

Little more I have to tell. Slowly I came back to my former strength, with a darling wife and good victuals. As for Lorna, she never tired of sitting and watching me eat and eat. And such is her heart, that she never tires of being with me here and there, among the beautiful places, and talking with her arm around me – so far at least as it can go, though half of mine may go round her – of the many fears, and troubles, dangers and discouragements, and worst of all the bitter partings, which we were forced to undergo.

R D BLACKMORE

Lorna Doone

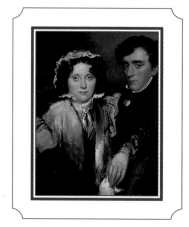

There is no more lovely, friendly and charming relationship, communion or company than a good marriage.

MARTIN LUTHER

Through the vales to my love!
To the happy small nest of home
Green from basement to roof;
Where the honey-bees come
To the window-sill flowers,
    And dive from above,
Safe from the spider that weaves
    Her warp and her woof
    In some outermost leaves.

Through the vales to my love!
Where the turf is so soft to the feet
    And the thyme makes it sweet,
    And the stately foxglove
Hangs silent its exquisite bells;
    And where water wells
The greenness grows greener,
    And bulrushes stand
Round a lily to screen her.

Nevertheless, if this land,
Like a garden to smell and to sight,
Were turned to a desert of sand;
    Stripped bare of delight,
    All its best gone to worst,
    For my feet no repose,
No water to comfort my thirst,
And heaven like a furnace above, –
    The desert would be
As gushing of waters to me,
The wilderness be as a rose,
    If it led me to thee,
    O my love.

CHRISTINA ROSSETTI

"A Bride Song"

*L*et me not to the marriage of true minds
Admit impediments; love is not love
Which alters when it alteration finds,
Or bends with the remover to remove.
O, no! it is an ever-fixed mark,
That looks on tempests and is never shaken;
It is the star to every wandering bark,
Whose worth's unknown, although his height be taken.
Love's not Time's fool, though rosy lips and cheeks
Within his bending sickle's compass come;
Love alters not with his brief hours and weeks,
But bears it out even to the edge of doom.
If this be error, and upon me proved,
I never writ, nor no man ever loved.

WILLIAM SHAKESPEARE
Sonnet number three

Annie of Tharaw, my true love of old,
She is my life, and my goods, and my gold.
Annie of Tharaw, her heart once again
To me has surrendered in joy and in pain.
Annie of Tharaw, my riches, my good,
Thou, O my soul, my flesh, and my blood!
Then come the wild weather, come sleet or come snow,
We will stand by each other, however it blow.
Oppression, and sickness, and sorrow, and pain
Shall be to our true love as links to the chain.
As the palm-tree standeth so straight and so tall,
The more the hail beats, and the more the rains fall –
So love in our hearts shall grow mighty and strong,
Through crosses, through sorrows, through manifold wrong . . .
How in the turmoil of life can love stand,
Where there is not one heart, and one mouth, and one hand?
Some seek for dissension, and trouble, and strife;
Like a dog and a cat live such man and wife.
Annie of Tharaw, such is not our love;
Thou art my lambkin, my chick, and my dove.
Whate'er my desire is, in thine may be seen;
I am king of the household, and thou art its queen.

HENRY WADSWORTH LONGFELLOW

"Annie of Tharaw"
from *The Low German of Simon Dach*

Trusty, dusky, vivid, true,
With eyes of gold and bramble-dew,
Steel-true and blade-straight,
The great artificer
Made my mate.

Honour, anger, valour, fire;
A love that life could never tire,
Death quench or evil stir,
The mighty master
Gave to her.

Teacher, tender, comrade, wife,
A fellow-farer true through life,
Heart-whole and soul-free,
The august father
Gave to me.

R L STEVENSON
"My Wife"

*M*y children, the offspring of temperance, as they were educated without softness, so they were at once well-formed and healthy; my sons hardy and active, my daughters beautiful and blooming.

It would be fruitless to deny exultation when I saw my little ones about me; but the vanity and the satisfaction of my wife were even greater than mine. When our visitors would say, "Well, upon my word, Mrs Primrose, you have the finest children in the whole country." – "Ay, neighbour," she would answer, "they are as Heaven made them – handsome enough, if they be good enough; for handsome is that handsome does." And then she would bid the girls hold up their heads; who, to conceal nothing, were certainly very handsome.

OLIVER GOLDSMITH
The Vicar of Wakefield

*H*ail wedded love! mysterious law, true source
Of human offspring, sole propriety
In Paradise of all things common else.
By thee adulterous lust was driv'n from men
Among the bestial herds to range; by thee
Founded in reason, loyal, just, and pure,
Relations dear, and all the charities
Of father, son, and brother, first were known.
Far be it, that I should write thee sin or blame,
Or think thee unbefitting holiest place,
Perpetual fountain of domestic sweets,
Whose bed is undefiled and chaste pronounced,
Present, or past, as saints and patriarchs used.
Here Love his golden shafts employs, here lights
His constant lamp, and waves his purple wings.
Reigns here and revels; not in the bought smile
Of harlots, loveless, joyless, unendeared,
Casual fruition; nor in court amours,
Mixed dance, or wanton mask, or midnight ball,
Or serenade, which the starved lover sings
To his proud fair, best quitted with disdain.
These, lulled by nightingales, embracing slept,
And on their naked limbs the flowery roof
Showered roses, which the morn repaired. Sleep on,
Blest pair, and O! yet happiest if ye seek
No happier state, and know to know no more.

JOHN MILTON
Paradise Lost

*A*fter a youth and manhood passed half in unutterable misery and half in dreary solitude, I have for the first time found what I can truly love – I have found you. You are my sympathy – my better self – my good angel – I am bound to you with a strong attachment. I think you good, gifted, lovely: a fervent, a solemn passion is conceived in my heart; it leans to you, draws you to my centre and spring of life, wraps my existence about you – and, kindling in pure and powerful flame, fuses you and me in one. It was because I felt and knew this, that I resolved to marry you.

CHARLOTTE BRONTE

Jane Eyre

If ever two were one, then surely we.
If ever man were loved by wife, then thee;
If ever wife was happy in a man,
Compare with me ye women if you can.
I prize thy love more than whole mines of gold,
Or all the riches that the East doth hold.
My love is such that rivers cannot quench,
Nor aught but love from thee give recompense.
Thy love is such I can no way repay,
The heavens reward thee manifold I pray.
Then while we live, in love let's so persevere,
That when we live no more, we may live ever.

ANNE BRADSTREET

"To My Dear and Loving Husband"

ACKNOWLEDGMENTS

The following pictures are reproduced with kind permission of the Visual Arts Library, London:
p1: Christmas Card, 19th cent, Victoria and Albert Museum. p6: *The Courtier Lover* by J Baptiste Pater, 18th cent. p7: *The Declaration* attributed to Henry Singleton. p8: *Portrait of a Couple* by François Guerin. p9: *Angelica Catalani* by Vigee Le-Brun. p10: *Sylvia* by Edwin Abbey. p11: *The Engagement of Raphael with the niece of Cardinal Bibiena* by Ingres, Walters Art Gallery. p12: *The Farewell* by C Spitzweg. p14: *Princess Radziwill* by Vigee Le-Brun, Paris. p15: *Wet Sunday Morning* by Edmund Blair Leighton. p16: *Lovers Under a Blossom Tree* by J Horsley, Philadelphia Museum of Art. p17: *The Lovers* by von Margitan. p18: *The Lovers or The Harvesters* by George Richmond, Edimedia/Phillips Fine Art Auctioneer. p19: *Harvest Time* by Julien Dupré. p21: *The Marriage* by G E Hicks, Geffrye Museum, London. p26: *When the Flowers Return* by Sir Lawrence Alma-Tadema, Leicester Galleries, London. p30: *Ophelia* by A Hughes, Toledo Museum of Art. p31: *La Bella Mano* by Dante Gabriel Rosetti, Delaware Art Museum, Samuel and Mary R Bancroft Memorial. p32: *The Medici Cycle: Marriage between Maria de Medici and Henri IV on 5th October 1600* by Rubens, Louvre, Paris. p37: *The Music* by Elisabeth Sonrel. p38: *The Soldier's Return* by Francis Wheatley. p40(l): *The Wedding Meal* by A Klipov. p40(r): *Wedding Meal* by A Vatazin. p44: *Dance and Games in the Garden* by M von Schwind, Vienna Osterr. Gallery. p48: *The Crown of White Flowers* by Elisabeth Sonrel. p49: *Lady Lilith* by Dante Gabriel Rossetti, Delaware Art Museum, Wilmington, Samuel and Mary R Bancroft Memorial. p54: *Couple* by Soien Lassoe Lange. p55: *Portrait of a Lady* by F H Mulard, Kimbell Museum of Art, Fort Worth. p56: *Family Bliss* by W Winner, Philadelphia Museum of Art. p57: *The Baillie Family* by Thomas Gainsborough, Tate Gallery, London. p60: *A Couple* attributed to Ittenbach, Louvre, Paris. p61: *The Enjoyable Awakening* by Albert Chevalia Taylor. p62: *In the Winter Garden* by Edouard Manet, National Gallery, Berlin.

From the Bridgeman Art Library, London: p2: *Signing the Marriage Register* by James Charles, Bradford Art Galleries and Museums. p3: "Here Comes the Bride", *The Wedding of George and Martha Washington in 1759* by J L Ferris, private collection. p4: *The Bride at Her Toilet* by Sir David Wilkie, National Gallery of Scotland, Edinburgh. p5: *The Wedding Breakfast* by Frederick Daniel Hardy, Atkinson Art Gallery, Southport, Lancs. p13: *The Huguenot* by Sir John Everett Millais, private collection. p20: *Wedding Bells* by James Hayllar, John Noott Galleries, Broadway, Worcs. p 25: *Signing the Register* by Edmund Blair Leighton, City of Bristol Museum and Art Gallery. p27: *The Honeymoon* by Sir Lawrence Alma-Tadema, private collection. p29: *The Seamstress* by Charles Baugniet, Victoria and Albert Museum. p33: *The Wedding Party* by Carl Herpfer, Christie's, London. p35: *None but the Brave Deserve the Fair* by J Shaw Compton, 19th cent, A & F Pears Ltd, London. p36: *The Wedding* by V Marais Milton, 19th cent, Eaton Gallery, Princes Arcade, London. p39: *The Village Wedding* by Sir Luke Fildes, Christopher Wood Gallery, London. p41: *The Wedding Meal at Yport* by Albert-Auguste Fourie, Musée des Beaux-Arts, Rouen. p43: *The Only Daughter* by James Hayllar, Forbes Magazine Collection, New York. p45: *The Cloakroom, Clifton Assembly Rooms* by Rolinda Sharples, City of Bristol Museum and Art Gallery. p46: *John Gibson Lockhart, biographer and son-in-law of Sir Walter Scott, and his wife Charlotte Sophia Scott* by Robert Scott Lauder, Scottish National Portrait Gallery, Edinburgh. p47: *Tess of the D'Urbervilles/The Elopement* by William Hatherell, private collection. p50: *Mated* by Marcus Stone, York City Art Gallery. p53: *Portrait of a Man and His Wife* by Cornelis de Vos, Rafael Valls Gallery, London. p58: *A Family Group* by John Downman, Agnew & Sons, London. p63: *The Lovers* by Pierre Auguste Renoir, Narodni Gallery, Prague.

From Lauros-Giraudon/The Bridgeman Art Library, London: p28: *The Bride*, engraved by J Battannier after Henri Lafon, Musée Carnavalet, Paris.